I0708039

An Alphabet of Place

The Little Snake River Valley

Sharon Salisbury O'Toole

Illustrations by
Martha Ann Kennedy

Cover photo by Pat Danscen

ISBN: 9798738833939

"Storytelling is a form of mapping: it connects the self to the self, people to people, and people to places over time…. Without unifying stories, we can become disconnected from ourselves, our loved ones, our history and our surroundings."

Kathryn Aalto, *Writing Wild—Women Poets, Ramblers and Mavericks Who Shape How We See the Natural World*

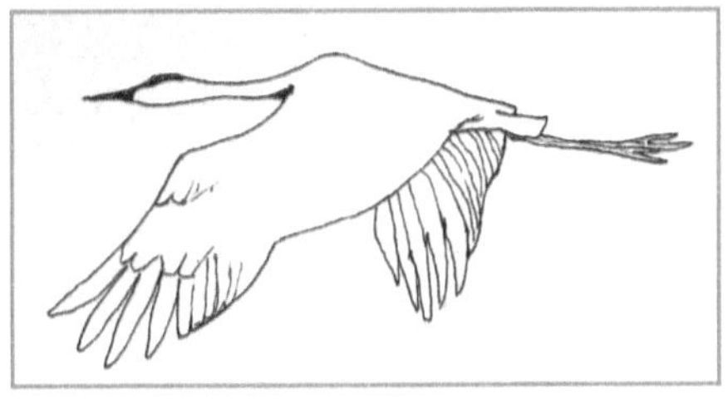

MCKENNEDY 2021

About the Author

Sharon Salisbury O'Toole is a rancher, writer and poet. She and her family operate the Ladder Ranch, which lies in the borderlands between Wyoming and Colorado along the Little Snake River. Sharon and her husband Pat like to say they raise "cattle, sheep, horses, dogs and children." Their grandchildren are the sixth generation on the same landscape. The Ladder Ranch website is: www.ladderranch.com. Go to "Ranch News" for a blog on life at the Ladder Ranch.

About the Illustrator

Martha Ann Kennedy has been an artist all her life. She lives and shows her work in Colorado's mesmeric San Luis Valley. She loves oil painting but enjoys working in just about any medium. You can see her work on her website www.martha-kennedy.com

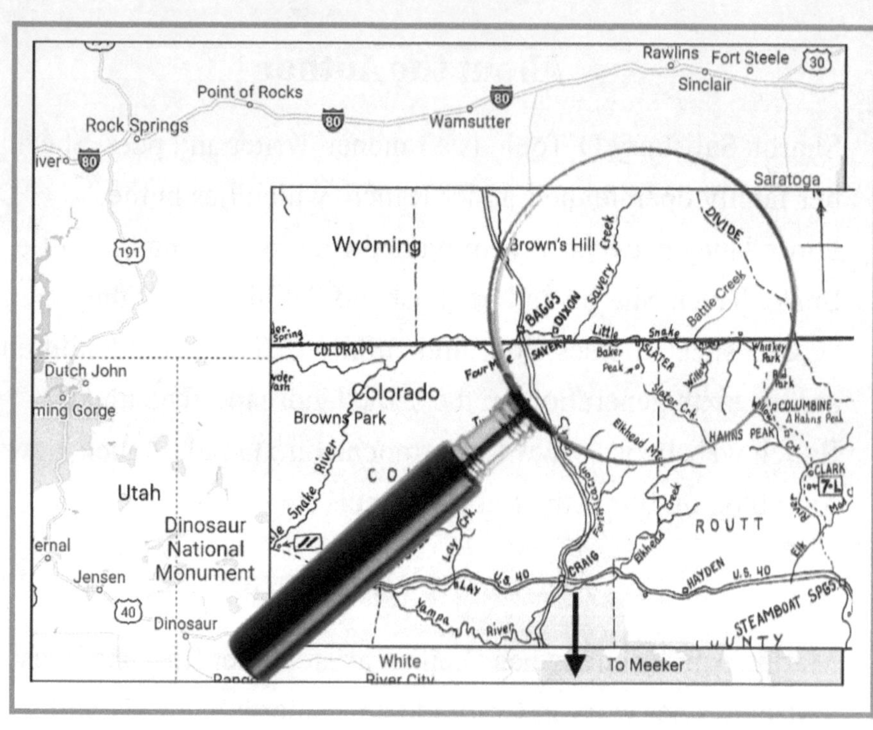

Rawlins
Fort Steele
30
Sinclair
Point of Rocks
80
Saratoga
Rock Springs
Wamsutter
DIVIDE
iver
80
Wyoming
Brown's Hill
Creek
191
Savery
Battle Creek
BAGGS
DIXON
Little
Snake
er.
Spring
COLORADO
Baker
Whiskey
Dutch John
Peak
SLATER
Park
ming Gorge
der
Willow
ash
Slater Crk.
Bad
Colorado
COLUMBINE
Park
Browns Park
Four M.
Hahns Peak
Elkhead Mtn.
HAHNS PEAK
C O
CLARK
Utah
Snake River
7-L
Dinosaur
Fortif.
ROUTT
ernal
National
Lay Crk.
Creek
Elkhead
Monument
Elkhead Creek
HAYDEN
U.S. 40
Elk
Jensen
U.S. 40
CRAIG
40
STEAMBOAT SPGS.
Dinosaur
Yampa
River
UUNTY
White
To Meeker
Rang
River City

Introduction:

An Alphabet of Place: The Little Snake River Valley is a celebration of my home, a remote mountain valley northwest of Steamboat Springs, Colorado and southwest of Rawlins, Wyoming, along the Wyoming/Colorado state line. "Alphabet" was inspired by an essay in the *Kenyon Review* by writer Alison Townsend—"An Alphabet of Here: A Wisconsin Prairie Sampler." I decided to create the ABCs of my valley. Each letter describes a critter, a plant, a place or historical characters (and characters they were!) at first generally, then more specifically and finally personally. I hope you enjoy reading it as much as I enjoyed writing it.

Thanks to those who helped me research, including local historians Linda Fleming and Bill Stocks. Thanks to the Little Snake River Museum staffers Lela Emmons and Elizabeth Campbell. Thanks to my daughter, Bridget, who was there at the beginning and the end. She did a lot of proofreading. And thanks to illustrator Martha Kennedy, who created the beautiful ink drawings, sometimes more than once. Martha also contributed her talents as an editor and book designer. It has been a labor of love for all of us!

A is for Antelope, as the creature is known in the American West. But the speedy ungulate is neither antelope nor goat, though it's called by both names. It is not even a member of the antelope family, but it is more correctly known as the pronghorn (*antilocapra americana*). The pronghorn is the fastest North American land animal and a ubiquitous dweller of the sagebrush steppe. Their herds have a sentinel who watches for predators while the others graze. When I was a child, antelope were inhabitants of the plains. With drought and incursion from humans, they have expanded their habitat to foothills and mountains. These wary animals have overcome their fear of closed spaces, like trees, to increase their access to forage and water. Our winter sheep country on the Red Desert includes the Chain Lakes Wildlife Habitat Management Area, critical winter habitat for antelope. Antelope do not migrate by instinct. They learn the route as they trail with their mothers. Some follow the same trail as our sheep, as they move from winter desert country to spring lambing (and kidding) grounds to summer forest. The antelope are our neighbors, summer and winter. Even after all these years, I look with wonder and respect when I happen across them in high mountain meadows, wary but well-fed.

B is for Bastion Mountain. Bastion was the original name of Battle Mountain, given by white trappers and settlers in the Little Snake River Valley along the present-day Wyoming/Colorado border. It is a massive volcanic mesa, dominating the landscape. It has the unique quality of looking the same from every ordinal direction—an immense butte in the shape of a loaf. Our mountain landscape was formed through volcanic eruptions millions of years ago, which left behind uniquely shaped formations. Battle Mountain's block-like shape is interrupted by a huge canyon on the east side where an explosion blew it out millennia ago. Bastion Mountain became Battle Mountain after an 1841 battle between American Indians—Arapaho, Sioux and Cheyenne—and a band of trappers, led by Henry Fraeb. The dispute involved the ownership of certain horses. It left a landscape of place names, including Battle Mountain, Battle Creek, Battle Lake and Squaw Mountain. In 2020, Colorado appointed a Geographic Naming Advisory Board to evaluate places with politically incorrect names. In our family, we discuss what would be an appropriate name for Squaw Mountain, which legend says sheltered the Shoshone wives and children of the trappers during the battle. I wish we knew the native names for Bastion/Battle, for Squaw Mountain and for all the distinctive volcanic features in our landscape.

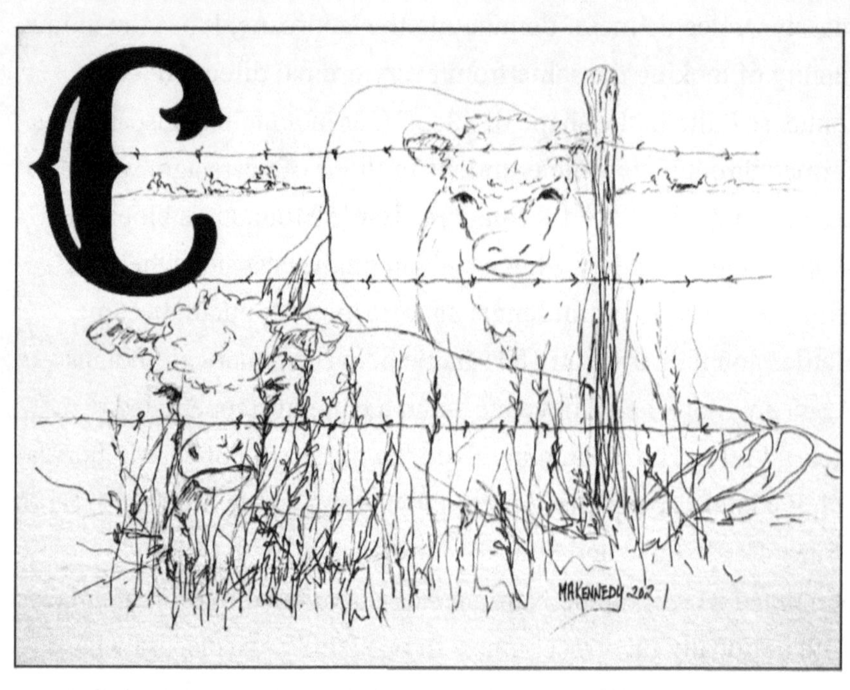

C is for Cow, the domestic animal whose superpower is to convert grass and sunshine into high-quality protein. Cows not only provide us with tasty and nutritious meat, but they also give us milk, cheese and other dairy products. Lots of by-products from leather to insulin to cosmetics also come to us from these versatile creatures. Properly managed, their grazing and hoof action works to capture carbon and restore damaged rangelands. George and Maggie Baggs brought the first cattle to the Valley in 1873, around the same time cattle arrived in Brown's Park—our geographical neighbor to the west. Cattle brought cattle rustling, a persistent problem. Local cattlemen formed the Snake River Stock Growers Association and aligned with Brown's Park most prominent graziers, including Ora Haley and Charlie Ayer. In 1900, the group reportedly hired Tom Horn as a "range detective." Shortly after, two popular Brown's Park ranchers, Matt Rash and Isom Dart, were shot and killed. Horn was not convicted for these killings. Rash and Dart may or may not have been guilty, but the rustling ceased, at least for a time. Cattle ranching is still an important part of the area economy and is a key part of local culture and identity. My earliest memories include following cows on horseback, the scent of sage rising, snuggled into my father's chest; calves following their moms, me feeling safe and proud—all of us doing our jobs.

D, of course, is for Dog. Throughout time, dogs have been our most faithful companions, our helpmates and sometimes our trickster adversaries. The native people who frequented the

Valley were accompanied by dogs, as were the trappers and the settlers. Today, we mostly see herding dogs, like Border collies and cattle dogs, as they help the ranchers tend their cattle and sheep. We also see livestock guardian dogs, known fondly as "Big White Dogs." Imports from the mountainous regions of Europe and Eurasia, their duty is to protect livestock from predators. Independent and smart, these guardians provide some peace of mind to livestock and livestock producers. Often they are discouraging, sometimes fatally, to their fellow canines—those wily and ever-hungry coyotes. Our

ranch had the first livestock guardian dogs in Wyoming, beginning with a Komondor, Noodles, who inspired me to write a children's book, "Noodles, Sheep Security Guard."

E is for Eagles, both bald and golden. The Valley has lots of them, along with a plethora of other raptors. Bald eagles are about the same size as Golden eagles, but they are not as strong when choosing and attacking prey, which include fish, rabbits and baby lambs. Eagles are also carrion eaters or scavengers, sometimes chasing other predators away from a tasty roadkill treat. Bald eagles mate for life and build nests atop tall trees. We often see them perched on the Dolan Mesa between the towns of Dixon and Savery and nesting along Battle Creek, which is an Audubon Important Bird Area. The road north of Dixon leads to our lambing grounds and runs high up on a steep hillside above Cottonwood Creek, another tributary of the Little Snake River. We used to watch an eagle's nest at eye level because the birds made their home in the branches of a cottonwood tree growing up from the stream bank below. Each spring, we enjoyed a roadside view of the eggs in the nest hatching into eaglets. Over the years, we had to look upward to see the nest as the tree grew. My dad would throw the carcasses of lambs, dead from birth or accident, to the bottom of the tree. His reasoning was that if the eagles had plenty to eat, they'd leave the live lambs, just up the creek, alone. Beavers felled the tree a few years ago, the cycle of nature continuing on.

F is for Forest, as in the great forest that lies on the headwaters of the Little Snake. It's now called the Medicine Bow National Forest in Wyoming and the Routt National Forest in Colorado, but it is one landscape. Elk, deer and antelope make their seasonal home in the forest, as they migrate to the high country on their transhumance journey for summer grazing. It hosts thousands of recreationists, who enjoy it for activities from camping to bicycle racing. This forest is also a working landscape. Its grasses sustain our livestock in the summer months, providing nutritious forage for cows and sheep while their grazing reduces danger from wildfires. It saw miners seeking copper on Haggerty Creek and gold near Hahn's Peak. It provided timber to mills in Colorado and Wyoming, and still does in smaller quantities. Today, much of the mill-bound timber is from trees killed by ravenous pine beetles. Now millions of acres are red and dead, and an ominous tinderbox. We have had to evacuate sheep from the Hinman Fire and cows from the Big Red Fire. We know it will burn—just not which part and which year.

G is for Greater Sage Grouse. Greater Sage Grouse represent an iconic species in the West. They are a species of dancing birds, known for their elaborate courting ritual, involving the males strutting on bare ground, puffing their chests and hooting, trying to lure the shy, or bored, females from their shelter in the surrounding sage. Habitat for Greater Sage Grouse is scattered throughout the Western sagebrush steppe, and the birds are considered an indicator species for the health of the sagebrush landscape. The birds are conservative and do not like change. They do not like the roads and activity that come with energy development. Greater Sage Grouse are particularly sensitive to wind towers and will not live near them since they perceive them as perches for predatory birds like eagles and hawks. We raise young grouse as well as young lambs. Large leks (dancing grounds) are located on our lambing grounds, where our springtime predator control allows the hens to nest and raise their young. In the summer, the hens and chicks have unfettered access to the wet meadows by the creek, as we rest the land from livestock grazing. Each April, third grade students from the Little Snake River Valley school go on an early morning field trip to watch the grouse dance and learn their ways. It is unforgettable!

H is for Hill, Brown's Hill that is. "Hill" does not do justice to the high and rambling plateau that is Brown's Hill. It also doesn't do justice to the once-thriving community that called it home. The hill lies several miles north of Dixon. It once represented hope to homesteaders who set about raising wheat. The small society boasted two schools and hosted many a dance. Drought and the Great Depression emptied the farms and scattered the residents. This landscape is mostly deserted now, save for a few summer cabins, seasonal grazing by cattle and sheep, deer and antelope. My grandmother's uncle died on Brown's Hill. The family was enjoying a summer picnic, when their automobile started rolling downhill. Uncle John threw himself in front of the machine, killing him and their young daughter Lillian. His widow, Nettie, was left with five children to raise. My family is among those who graze livestock on Brown's Hill in the spring and fall. Summers we leave to the deer and antelope.

I is for Immigrants. The earliest Euro-Americans in the Valley were French trappers. Others followed, first trapping beaver and trading with the local American Indian communities. When the beaver trade faded, they harvested and bartered for buffalo hides and meat. For almost a half century, trappers and travelers, as well as the transient natives, existed in the in-between time—after the first trappers and explorers came into the country and before white settlers came to stay—trading and marrying. Later settlers came to raise livestock, especially after the Union Pacific rail line was completed in 1865, giving access to Eastern markets. Many of the residents today are descendants of the original immigrants from Europe in the 1880s. These hopeful immigrants mostly came from Ireland, Scotland and England. Some are related to Mormon settlers, who often were of Scandinavian descent. Some families, then and now, immigrated to the Valley from Mexico and New Mexico. Others descend from intermarriages with American Indians, mostly Shoshone. Folks are still drawn by the beautiful scenery, abundant wildlife and a chance to begin anew. Some marry into long-settled families. As my grandparents told my father when he left for college, "It's fine to get an education, son, but find a wife you're not related to!" Luckily for me and for many, he found my mom, Laura.

Little Snake River Museum
P.O. Box 13
Savery WY
82332

J is for John Charles Fremont (sorry Jim Baker, but you appear elsewhere). Fremont was a giant in the history of the West. Wyoming and Colorado both named counties for Fremont, who was a military man, an explorer and mapmaker, and the first governor of California. Fremont's travels took him through the Valley in 1844. He reported that the party "…took our way across the hills, where every hollow had a spring of running water, with good grass." Ahead of them were the "…high mountains which divide the Pacific from the Mississippi waters," and "…entering here among the lower spurs, or foothills of the range, the face of the country began to improve with a magical rapidity… The country here appeared more variously stocked with game than any part of the Rocky Mountains we had visited; and its abundance is owing to the excellent pasturage, and its dangerous character as a war ground." Fremont's words live on because his wife, Jessie Benton Fremont, wrote of his travels years later, to support the family. I have often quoted Fremont's words, which still ring true, about both the "excellent pasturage" and the "dangerous character."

K
Prayer Fence
All are Welcome to tie a Ribbon
ARK-Amazing River Kids
WYOMING
MKENNEDY 2021

K is for Kids. The Amazing River Kids program is a type of "Sunday School," held on Thursdays after school at St. Paul's Episcopal Church in Dixon. ARK welcomes children of all denominations to participate in the program, and kids from all faith groups eagerly look forward to the program. Each session begins with snacks, a Bible story told by one of the leaders and discussion in the chapel, followed by singing and a craft related to the Bible story. A common theme is God's love for all children. ARK youngsters present the annual Christmas pageant for the community. My grandkids have all participated, and played, variously, a shepherd, a sheep, a cow, a king, the innkeeper, and even Mary in the Christmas program, which always plays to a packed house. An annual activity takes place prior to Memorial Day, and before the ARK program disbands for the summer. It is a visit to the Reader Cemetery, where the kids place pinwheels on the children's graves. It teaches them about the past and makes the cemetery a place to celebrate our Valley's rich history. Little Lillian Terrill (see "H") lies in one of the graves they decorate and honor.

MAKENNEDY
2021

L is for Little Snake River—what else? The Little Snake River is an actual river, the name of the valley it flows through and the name of the community it supports. The Little Snake flows into the Yampa which flows into the Green which flows into the Colorado. The river flows for about 155 miles (249 km), crossing the Wyoming/Colorado state line 31 times. It passes near Slater, Colorado, and Savery, Dixon and Baggs, Wyoming, before flowing west to the Arambel Place and turning south at the River Bridge. It waters our Valley and confounds water managers in both states. The River provides a fishery and irrigation water for high altitude hay and alfalfa. The flood irrigation feeds wetlands, providing habitat for birds and other wildlife, and recharges groundwater. Some high tributaries are diverted to provide water for Cheyenne, on the Eastern Slope. Locals are protective of water and water rights, as thirsty downstream interests constantly seek supplies. The community is known in the area as The River, as in "Are you from The River?" Yes, I am.

M is for Maggie Baggs—the more notorious half of the couple for whom the town of Baggs was named. In 1872, Maggie and her cowman husband George first visited Brown's Park, to the west of the Valley on the Colorado/Utah/Wyoming border. She was reported to be the second white woman to set foot there. The following year, George and Maggie brought in a herd of cattle wearing the Double Eleven brand and established pasturage on what is now the townsite of Baggs, along the banks of the Little Snake River. It is said that George was patient and long-suffering, while Maggie, who preferred horseback work to domesticity, had an eye for their Double Eleven cowboys. Finally, George and Maggie divorced and Maggie won a settlement based on the money earned from the cattle. Two geographic landmarks, Maggie's Nipple to the east and Nipple Peak to the west, were named for her. When she learned of the naming, she reportedly roped the guilty cowhand and dragged him down the street behind her horse. In a poetic history of the Little Snake, "The Ballad of Maggie Baggs," I wrote, "In fact, a mountain bears my name, its christening caused quite a ripple. This lovely peak, just up the creek, is known as 'Maggie's. . . Mountain'."

DR. NOYES, M.D.

N is for Noyes, as in Doctor Noyes. Dr. Edmond Noyes was the only physician to make a permanent home in the Valley. A native of New York City, his family had a plantation in Jamaica. He moved west and started his practice in the Valley around the turn of the last century. Local lore holds that some of his first clients were outlaws from the Hole-in-the-Wall Gang, who abducted him to care for the wounded. After tending to the outlaws, he was released. When asked about the adventure, he would smile, and neither confirm nor deny. Dr. Noyes had the good luck and good sense to marry a skilled nurse, Savilla Garrish, 22 years his junior. The pair cared for the people of the community until the 1950s, and they assisted in the delivery of around 1,100 babies. The birth records are on display at the local museum. Their famous "Noyes Burn Salve" is still sold today by their descendants, who keep the formula secret. My grandmother, Emma, was a midwife who sometimes assisted Dr. and Mrs. Noyes. Dr. Noyes reportedly arrived shortly after the home birth of my father, George.

O is for Oil and Gas. The energy production industry has been part and parcel of the Valley's economy for decades. Many ranches have stayed in business due to the income brought in as locals worked in the energy fields. Oil and natural gas are abundant in the area, and its infrastructure dots the landscape. Royalties from energy production support education and local districts including the Conservation District, the Health Care District, the Solid Waste District and the cemeteries. The first discovery is credited to Wiff Wilson, a cattleman, homestead locator and entrepreneur. In 1925, he discovered the gas field near Powder Wash, west of Baggs. His homestead there is part of our ranch today. The same inland seas that laid down the precursors of petroleum products also laid coal beds under much of the Valley. Small coal mines used to dot the landscape, especially near Savery Creek, to supply needed heat for the winter. We still see exposed seams in road-cuts and bluff sides.

M.A.KENNEDY
2021
P

P is for Poor Farm, once located just west of the town of Dixon. A Wyoming statute directed that the sole responsibility for the relief of the indigent, the care of the sick and the aged and the burial of paupers was borne by the Board of County Commissioners. It served Carbon County from 1911 to 1935. More than 36 different county residents resided there during that time, with some making it their home for more than a decade. Many spent their last years at the Poor Farm. Twenty-three funerals were conducted from the Episcopal Church for "Riverside Home residents." Most were buried at the Poor Farm Cemetery, northwest of Dixon. My father recalled watching the flames as the Poor Farm, which was a repurposed hotel, burned. His Aunt Nettie, the widow of John (see H), managed the Poor Farm. She rushed to the Dixon school, where Dad and several cousins were students. She called for the "big boys" to fight the fire. He recounted that he and the other "little kids" responded as well. No use. The building was a complete loss. The system was replaced by social security, Medicaid and "retirement homes." I'm not sure it was an ideal solution.

Q is for Quaking Aspen, or *Populus Tremuloides*, which do indeed tremble and quake. In the summer, the leaves murmur in the breeze. In the fall, the bright yellow leaves make quite a racket as wind shakes and plucks them and sends their colorful leaves to the forest floor. Aspens thrive in the widest natural range in North America, both in latitude and longitude. Aspens grow in "clones," sending up buds from their spreading root systems. The distinctive white bark continues photosynthesis through the winter months. A much-photographed passage is known as "Aspen Alley," where the trees form a tunnel on the road north through the Medicine Bow Forest. Their soft bark forms a palette for sheepherders, hunters and lovers, who carve "arborglyphs" into their trunks. The common themes are names, dates and mildly pornographic art. My father called a stretch of the Savery Stock Driveway near the Government Corrals the "Sheepherders' Hall of Fame."

R is for Reader Bugs! Reader bugs are uniquely named on the
Little Snake River, but elsewhere they are called Boxelder
bugs. Local lore has it that these ubiquitous insects are so
named because of their abundance at the Reader Place. The
Reader Place, or Stonewall Ranch, was the first homestead on
the Little Snake, established in 1871. Noah Reader, his wife
Rosanna (the first white woman in the Valley) and sons George,
William and Albert stopped in Rawlins for supplies, bound for
Montana. There they made the acquaintance of Bibleback
Brown (see X) who persuaded them to accompany him to the
Little Snake and settle. The desperate family did take up a
homestead there, and prospered. The young men found work in
the Hahn's Peak gold mines. Rosanna Graham Reader was
known as Medicine Woman to the Utes. She kept a horse
nearby, day and night, in case she needed to attend to an ailing
neighbor or stranger. The Readers were not discouraged by the
Reader bugs. Their name lives on today as this insect continues
to plague those in the area. I was in college before I knew that
others called them Boxelder bugs!

S is for Savery Stock Driveway. The Savery Stock Driveway was created as a partial response to the cattle and sheep wars around the turn of the last century. The "good pasturage" noted by John Fremont drew stock raisers seeking that pasture. Generally, the high deserts north of Baggs were controlled by sheepmen. Colorado was dominated by the cattle ranchers. Sheep producers wanted to profit from the good summer grazing in the nearby Colorado forests. After several skirmishes in which sheep and sheepherders were killed, the Wyoming sheepmen denied trailing rights to cattle growers who needed to cross to bring their animals to and from the railheads in Rawlins and Wamsutter. It was resolved when the Savery Stock Driveway and the Muddy Creek Driveway were designated, along with water holes, for the allocated passage of livestock. Ironically, many of the fought-over pasturages today see both cattle and sheep grazing. My own family grazes both species on several of these "battlegrounds," balancing their use and improving the rangeland resource.

MAKENNEDY 2021

T is for Trappers, who were integral to the "settlement" of the Little Snake River. Savery takes its name from Ceran St. Vrain, an early French trapper. The most famous of the area mountain men is Jim Baker, who lends his name to Bakers Peak. His career included stints as frontiersman, trapper, hunter, fur trader, explorer, army scout, interpreter, soldier, territorial militia officer, rancher, mine owner, toll keeper and, of course, mountain man. Baker trapped beaver and scouted with Jim Bridger, Kit Carson and John Fremont. He was famously dispatched by Jim Bridger to warn Henry Fraeb and his party of the impending attack by Arapaho, Sioux and Cheyenne warriors at their camp on today's Battle Creek (see B). Baker later said of Fraeb, "He was the ugliest dead man I ever saw, and I have seen a good many. . . When he was killed he never fell, but sat braced against a stump, a sight to behold". He married, successively, three Shoshone women—Marina, Mary and her sister Eliza—and fathered several children.He always returned to the Valley. His cabin, which featured a defense tower on top, is today located at the Little Snake River Museum in Savery. He was known as the "Red-Headed Shoshone" and "Honest Jim." Baker's descendants still live in the Valley. His contemporaries included Bill Slater, Bibleback Brown (see X) and Bob Dixon, who likewise live on as place names. His descendants are my friends and neighbors.

U is for Ute. The Northern Utes were one of several tribes that made their way through the Valley and used it as a summer hunting ground. Accounts tell of Utes and Shoshone, and the Sioux, Arapahoe, and Cheyenne from the Laramie plains. They too converged for the good pasturage and probably fought on the "dangerous war grounds" described by Fremont. As settlement increased, the natives were pushed to reservations. After the Utes were driven from their lands near Meeker, Colorado, following the Battle of Milk River, they were forced to move to a reservation in Utah, near present-day Vernal. The original boundaries, set by treaty, shrank as more settlers wanted the best country. Some tribal members, unhappy with Utah's harsh landscape, traveled to South Dakota, intending to make their home with the Sioux. This was a futile trek, for they were not welcomed by the Sioux nor the military. In 1908, they headed back to the Utah reservation, passing in sad caravans through Baggs. The native American presence is still to be found. Our ranch near Powder Wash is home to petroglyphs, teepee circles and countless artifacts from earlier times, many found near the live water of Lower Powder Spring. Sometimes the curtain is thin.

V is for Veterans. Much of the early history of the Valley is soaked with conflict. Following the Civil War, displaced soldiers and families headed west, seeking a new beginning. Some eventually ended up in the Valley. Soldiers who fought in various conflicts, including World War I, received "script" in lieu of wages, which they could use to claim land. Some veterans did use script to claim land when they settled in the Valley. Then and now, sons and daughters of the area continue to serve in the military. Their service is memorialized at the Little Snake River Museum in Savery where a monument is inscribed with the names of those who fulfilled this duty. All Army, Navy, Marine, Air Force and National Guard veterans who have ties to the community are included, from pioneers who fought in the Civil War and the Spanish American War to veterans of Iraq and Afghanistan. Each Veteran's Day, folks gather to remember and tell stories. Names are added as they are discovered. The inscribed names of my father, my aunt and uncle, and two nephews appear beside their fellow veterans.

WANTED
ROBERT LEROY PARKER
Alias
BUTCH CASSIDY
HARRY LONGBAUGH
Alias
THE SUNDANCE KID
$5,000
$5,000
REWARD
WILL BE PAID FOR THE
OF THESE FUG
DEAD O

W is for Wild Bunch, as in Butch Cassidy and the Wild Bunch. Baggs was a popular destination. The Wild Bunch celebrated in Baggs following their notorious train robberies along the Union Pacific line. The robbery at Tipton on June 29, 1900, netted either $50.45 or $55,000, depending upon the account. The bandits, led by the intelligent and charming Butch, whose given name was George LeRoy Parker, eluded law enforcement and decamped to Baggs to celebrate. They settled into the Bull Dog Saloon and shot up various fixtures and the bar. Before leaving town, they counted the damage and paid a dollar per bullet hole to the tolerant proprietor. Butch was well-liked among the local populace. "Butch Cassidy did more to redistribute wealth in Northwestern Colorado than Franklin Delano Roosevelt, and he did it a whole lot quicker and without any red tape," said one old-timer who recalled Butch and the gang. When I was a child, there were folks in Baggs who claimed he had come back in the 1920s to visit his old haunts.

$\mathbf{X}$ is for x-roads where time and place cross. The trappers came, drawn to the same hunting grounds favored and fought over by American Indians. Early trapper "Bibleback Brown" was reported to be stooped in stature and a devout reader and expounder of the Bible, hence the nickname. When he died, neighbors learned that his actual name was Henry Brockmire, (AKA John Brockmeyer). Brown's Hill and Bibleback Mountain near Slater memorialize him. Slater, Colorado, is named for Brown's long-time trapping partner, Bill Slater. The pair were drawn to the Valley by its rich abundance of beaver fur and other trapping opportunities. As time passed more settlers appeared, and the need for services such as mail delivery increased. Local rancher Bob Dixon accepted the job to handle the mail. After Dixon's unexpected death, storekeeper and trader Charlie Perkins, a man known to bend the rules, took over the route without informing the government. When the authorities learned of the situation, they kept Perkins on the job, since the mail was being delivered in an orderly manner. They did, however, keep the name of Dixon for the post office. Dixon today has a post office, a church, a hotel and a bar, where folks still cross paths. Crossing the landscape too, are the great migrations of deer, elk, antelope and birds such as geese, ducks, and the Sandhill Crane. Some cranes pass through and some over-summer. I welcome the arrival of the cranes as the first sign of spring, as the mated pairs show up while snow is still on the ground.

Y is for Yummy. Since time immemorial, the denizens of the Valley have survived and mostly thrived on the bounty of fish, big game and even some birds. The Little Snake River and its tributaries host several tasty fish species, including the Wyoming state fish—the Cutthroat trout, and the migratory Kokanee salmon. The Baggs deer herd is famous nationwide among hunters and photographers. Battle Mountain is known to elk hunters far and wide. The elk and antelope are abundant and thriving. Fall brings the retorts of gunshots and the twang of arrows as hunters, both local and visiting, fill their larders for the winter. My grandmother, who drove a Belgian draft horse team during haying season, told of hunting sage chickens (see G) as they were flushed from the fields, and frying them up for hungry hay hands. I can almost smell the cut hay and the sizzling hens.

Z is for zzzzzzz, the sound of warning created when a
"buzzworm" (rattlesnake) vibrates the tip of its tail.
Rattlesnakes and the Little Snake River Valley are intertwined.
The name of the river comes from its winding, twisting path,
from the headwaters in the Sierra Madres to its confluence with
the Yampa. The "Little" distinguishes it from Wyoming's larger
waterway, the Snake River, a tributary of the Columbia. Some
of its headwaters are diverted to the city of Cheyenne—the
only trans-mountain diversion in the state. Local wisdom holds
that rattlers are not found above Three Forks, where South
Fork, Middle Fork (King Solomon Creek) and Roaring Fork
come together to form the Little Snake. Downstream, actual
rattlesnakes are abundant in the warm months. They are to be
avoided — made easier by the snakes' warning, a blood-
chilling rattle. The mascot at the local K-12 school is — what
else?! — the Rattlers. My family members are all proud Little
Snake River Rattlers. Be warned!